The Fever Chart

Three Visions of the Middle East

One Short Sleepe

OTHER WORKS BY NAOMI WALLACE
PUBLISHED BY TCG

In the Heart of America and Other Plays
INCLUDES:

One Flea Spare
In the Heart of America
The War Boys
Slaughter City
The Trestle at Pope Lick Creek

The Fever Chart

Three Visions of the Middle East

With *One Short Sleepe*

Naomi Wallace

THEATRE COMMUNICATIONS GROUP
NEW YORK
2009

The Fever Chart: Three Visions of the Middle East and *One Short Sleepe*
are published by Theatre Communications Group, Inc., 520 Eighth Avenue,
24th Floor, New York, NY 10018–4156

This publication is made possible in part with public funds from the New York
State Council on the Arts, a State Agency.

TCG books are exclusively distributed to the book trade by Consortium Book
Sales and Distribution.

LIBRARY OF CONGRESS CATALOGING-IN-PUBLICATION DATA
Wallace, Naomi.
The fever chart : three visions of the Middle East, a play ; with One short sleepe
/ Naomi Wallace.—1st ed.
p. cm.
ISBN 978-1-55936-337-2
1. Jewish-Arab relations—Drama. 2. Middle East—Drama. I. Wallace, Naomi.
One short sleepe. II. Title.
PS3573.A42688F48 2009
812'.54—dc22   2009010206

Cover design by Lisa Govan
Cover art by Bruce McLeod
Text design and composition by Lisa Govan

First Edition, May 2009

For Mona and Rashid Khalidi

Contents

The Fever Chart

Three Visions of the Middle East

The Fever Chart: Three Visions of the Middle East
is based on true events.

Production History

Patrick Morris of Menagerie Theatre Company and Golden Thread Productions were instrumental in the development of *The Fever Chart: Three Visions of the Middle East.*

The Fever Chart: Three Visions of the Middle East was developed in Hartford Stage's 2006 Brand:NEW Festival. It was first workshopped at Mill Mountain Theatre's Norfolk Southern Festival of New Works, under the direction of David Gothard. *A State of Innocence (Vision One)* was commissioned by 7:84 Theatre Company of Scotland. *Between This Breath and You (Vision Two)* was written for the Hotbed Festival in Cambridge, U.K. *The Retreating World (Vision Three)* was commissioned by the McCarter Theatre Center.

The Fever Chart: Three Visions of the Middle East was produced in 2008 at New York's Public Theater (Oskar Eustis, Artistic Director; Mara Manus, Executive Director) as part of the Public Lab series. It was directed by Jo Bonney, with scenic design by Rachel Hauck, costume design by Ilona Somogyi, lighting design by Lap Chi Chu, sound design by Christian Frederickson; the production stage manager was Christina Lowe. The cast was:

Vision One: A State of Innocence

UM HISHAM QISHTA   Lameece Issaq
YUVAL   Arian Moayed
SHLOMO   Waleed F. Zuaiter

Vision Two: Between This Breath and You

MOURID KAMAL   Waleed F. Zuaiter
TANYA LANGER   Natalie Gold
SAMI ELBAZ   Arian Moayed

Vision Three: The Retreating World

ALI   Omar Metwally

Vision One

A State of Innocence

CHARACTERS

UM HISHAM QISHTA   Palestinian woman, from Rafah, late forties

YUVAL   Israeli soldier, from Tel Aviv, twenty-seven

SHLOMO   Israeli architect, elegant man, fifties

PLACE

Something like a small zoo, but more silent, empty, in Rafah, Palestine. Or a space that once dreamed it was a zoo.

TIME

2002.

NOTE

Characters often do not look directly at one another. It is as though they can see one another without eye contact.

Um Hisham enters, very focused. She takes a scarf and carefully, methodically, wraps her head in the scarf. She adjusts it until it's right; she is then ready for the vision to begin. Now she looks at Yuval.

Yuval is dressed as a zookeeper might be dressed, but still military, cleaning a large, simple cage, which might look like scaffolding. His uzi hangs near by. Um Hisham stands watching him at work. He is at first not aware of her. He speaks to us, the public:

YUVAL: I say to him when we're alone, I say: "He whom love touches not, walks in darkness." Do you, my friend? Do you walk in darkness? And then he winks at me. Ever had a porcupine wink at you? It's like the whole symposium's in that flick of a gesture. He knows. Damn it, he knows! And his name is Shadack Winko. And it's a small zoo too, but it's got a big spirit, and only two emus: Tricky Beak and Horton. Tricky Beak has only one eye and her beak's twisted. Her brother is Horton. Horton is . . . dull. Two camels. Dromedary. One's named Fairway and the other is Hoboken Bromwell. Then two ring-tailed cats, Buddy and Briggs. Three water buffalo: Chesterfield, Erkle and Alfalfa. And one puny monkey: Dingleberry Dibbit. And damn it, yes, I named every one of them from the scraps I picked up when we go back to the Big Apple every summer and visit family.

(Um Hisham has begun to softly sing a song in Arabic.)

But every morning I wake and an animal . . . No. But it's true. A different piece. It's back the next morning but then another part is gone again. There is something I don't know.

(He speaks in Hebrew: "Something is wrong with this zoo. God help us." Um Hisham's song can now clearly be heard.)

Excuse me but that's against the rules.

UM HISHAM: What is?

YUVAL: Gurgling.

UM HISHAM: I'm not gurgling. I'm singing.

YUVAL: Gurgling. Singing. Same thing. Not allowed in this zoo.

UM HISHAM: You don't have tortoises. Why don't you have tortoises?

YUVAL: Only the animals may sing and gurgle.

UM HISHAM: Where is the ostrich?

YUVAL: It's their home after all.

UM HISHAM: Where is the deer? Where is the kangaroo?

YUVAL: Would you like to see Shadack Winko? He's napping but I can wake him for you.

UM HISHAM: No. Let Winko sleep. And you should sleep, too.

YUVAL: Sleep? I'm the boss of this zoo. I need to stay alert.

UM HISHAM: Go away, Yuval.

YUVAL *(Threatening)*: Hey. How do you know my name, lady? Remember that *(Quotes)* "The one who comes to kill us, we shall rise early and kill him." I'm not afraid of you. Are you a terrorist?

UM HISHAM *(Playfully)*: Palestinorist. Terrestinian. Palerrorist. I was born in the country of Terrorist. I commit terrible acts of Palestinianism. I eat liberty from a bowl on the Wall. Fanatic. Security. Democracy.

YUVAL: Don't get playful with me. You want to throw me in the sea.

UM HISHAM: I just might. But I can't get to the sea. Seventeen and a half checkpoints keep me from it.

YUVAL *(In Hebrew)*: Would you shut up, woman, and leave me alone?

UM HISHAM: I would like to leave you alone.

YUVAL: You understand Hebrew?

UM HISHAM: How is your mother?

YUVAL: She doesn't like the zoo.

UM HISHAM: I've got something that belongs to her.

YUVAL *(Laughs)*: I don't think so, lady.

(Um Hisham removes her scarf, leaving it draped around her shoulders.)

UM HISHAM: I came to this zoo a few years ago. There was a small swimming pool.

(She looks for the place where the pool was, then finds it.)

Yes. It was here. I brought my daughter, Asma, here to swim.

YUVAL: There is no swimming pool here. Did you get a ticket when you came in?

UM HISHAM *(Discovering another spot)*: There were two slides here, near the bird aviary.

YUVAL: How do you know my mother?

UM HISHAM: I know it's hard to believe, looking at it now, but it was beautiful here.

(Shlomo hurries on, carrying a clipboard and a wooden box that holds his surveying equipment. He is a little confused by his surroundings, but puts down the box and begins to make notes. He gestures to Yuval.)

SHLOMO: You. Who are you? You in charge here?

YUVAL: Yes, sir.

SHLOMO: This place is full of holes. A veritable security clusterfuck as we say in the business.

YUVAL: What business?

SHLOMO: Anyone else here? Just the two of you then. *(Makes notes)* Nothing more sacred. Mother and son. Like the land and the settler—though the one's from Brooklyn . . . Don't get me started!

UM HISHAM: He is not—

YUVAL: She is not—

SHLOMO: An architect. But I am. And an architect is naturally a philosopher, *(To Yuval)* as you wish to be.

YUVAL: Yeah. I'm a grad student in philosophy from Tel Aviv University. How do—

SHLOMO: And this zoo is a disgrace to Zionist architecture.

UM HISHAM: My first house was destroyed in 1967—

SHLOMO: Was your house part of the Wall and Tower model?

UM HISHAM: No.

SHLOMO: I thought not.

(He proceeds to help Um Hisham onto the wooden box. He then links arms with Yuval, forming a "wall" around her "tower.")

The Homa Umigdal, the Wall and Tower, was our very first architectural model for the family home. Homa Umigdal! Homa Umigdal! Homa Umigdal!

YUVAL: He's mad.

SHLOMO: This model was the cradle of the nation, the very nest and egg that made the desert bloom.

(He and Yuval slowly rotate around Um Hisham.)

Circle the wagons, up with the periscope! Homa Umigdal—a prayer, a rhyme. And a spell.

(Shlomo gets Yuval to chant softly with him: "Homa Umigdal, Homa Umigdal, Homa Umigdal." Then he stops circling.)

Shhh. So, my good woman, what do you see?

(Um Hisham looks across the landscape.)

UM HISHAM: Palestinians.

SHLOMO: Exactly! And we are?

UM HISHAM: Lunatics.

SHLOMO: Protection. Homa Umigdal.

UM HISHAM: The model was a machine of invasion.

YUVAL: Yeah. I read about it at Oxford.

UM HISHAM: Nest and egg. Ha. Your Homa Umigdal houses had many little feet and they kept on coming. Another.

Another. *(She counts the little houses she imagines)* Another. Another. Another.

SHLOMO: Homa Umigdal! Since we cannot remove this zoo—

UM HISHAM: You can't remove this zoo. It's a ruin.

SHLOMO: I've made my living building on ruins. As I say, since we cannot remove this zoo to a hilltop, which is where one is truly safe, we shall have to squeeze it into the Homa Umigdal model.

UM HISHAM: And the animals?

SHLOMO: They will feel safer. Happier. The fear of a terrorist attack can put an animal off its food. Bad for business. I will propose to the government that each animal have a Wall and Tower.

YUVAL: Ever seen the penguin pool at London Zoo? Now that's archit—

SHLOMO: Exactly! But higher walls and a real tower.

YUVAL: But I read that the concrete walkway was hard on their feet.

SHLOMO: Security has its price.

(Shlomo begins to measure. Um Hisham sits on the box. Shlomo puts the measuring tape in her hand, with her arm up. As she holds the tape, he measures from her hand to the floor, in four directions.)

UM HISHAM: How will visitors see the penguins?

SHLOMO: Ah, but the penguins will be able to see the visitors, which is far more important.

YUVAL: We don't have any penguins. Can you do the Homa Umigdal for the porcupine?

SHLOMO: Of course. I'm an architect!

UM HISHAM: Where are the tortoises? Where is the ostrich? Where is the kangaroo?

YUVAL: How the hell should I know? I went to sleep on duty one afternoon and I woke up in this *(Curses in Hebrew)* zoo. Have you seen the animals in the morning? I run from cage to cage but it's darkness inside. And the noise. The camels are the worst. *(Makes the sound of a camel scream)* And I find pieces in the cages. Pieces of themselves. The emus are missing their toes. The ring-tailed cats have no tails. The water buffalo. Their long ribs have fallen out of their bodies so their sides have collapsed. And the monkey. I cannot speak of the monkey.

SHLOMO: I saw the monkey on my way in. He looked just fine.

YUVAL: But that's just it. By the afternoon the pieces have grown back, only to be torn away again each night.

SHLOMO: Now you are being dramatic.

UM HISHAM: It's true. I've seen it.

SHLOMO: Then believing is seeing. Like building.

(Um Hisham lets go of the end of the tape measure. It slaps the ground.)

(To Um Hisham) Where are we?

(Shlomo looks around, unsure. Um Hisham stares at him.)

YUVAL *(In Hebrew, panicked)*: Oh my God.

SHLOMO: Hey, I said where are we?

YUVAL *(In Hebrew)*: Oh my God. Oh my God. Oh my God.

(Shlomo slaps Yuval in the face to bring him around.)

SHLOMO: Snap out of it. Let's talk about . . . Tel Aviv? Huh?

YUVAL: Yeah. My folks came over from New York to Tel Aviv when they were kids.

SHLOMO: Yes. Let us start at the beginning? Tel Aviv is . . . ?

YUVAL: All right, all right . . . Borrowed from the Book of Ezekiel.

SHLOMO: And?

UM HISHAM: He doesn't know.

SHLOMO: Very likely the only city to be named after a book, Herzl's futuristic, and—

UM HISHAM: —not very good, novel *Altneuland*. First published—

SHLOMO: 1902, and translated as—

YUVAL: *Tel Aviv.*

SHLOMO: Yes. What useless facts we architects acquire.

UM HISHAM: Better than collecting facts on the ground: your illegal settlements.

SHLOMO: Your mother sounds like—

YUVAL: She's not—

UM HISHAM: I'm not—

SHLOMO *(Suddenly quotes, excited)*: "Move, run and grab as many hilltops as you can to enlarge the Jewish settlements because everything we take now will stay ours . . . everything we don't grab will go to them."

YUVAL: Ariel Sharon. Before he was prime min—

SHLOMO: That's right. But I am not like that overripe tic of a man. I do not confuse a hilltop with holiness.

UM HISHAM: I am a Palestinian. I am not his mother.

SHLOMO: Oh.

UM HISHAM: You with your building, building. You eat up our future.

YUVAL: And given the chance you would eat us.

SHLOMO: I do not eat anymore. I will be ninety-six years old in November.

YUVAL: What? You look barely forty.

UM HISHAM: The lies of an Israeli architect.

SHLOMO: I assure you I am indeed that old. I bathe in the Dead Sea. Each time I give it some of my dying.

UM HISHAM: You are a funny man, Shlomo, and at moments I am entertained. But I don't have time for you today. Leave us alone. Take your Wall and Tower with you.

YUVAL: She's right. This is no place for you. You give me chills.

SHLOMO: Charmed, I'm sure. Thank you, both. But I'm on official business. Of the utmost importance. No one stands in the way of architecture's path! So. I must redesign the zoo. And . . . and I am lonely. I have traveled so far. Ninety-six years! I was a Red Guard, you know, a proud soviet pioneer until the revolution began to eat its own. I was lucky to escape with my life. But the zealous survive! I was a zealous revolutionary, then a zealous agricultural expert in Birobidzhan, Siberia, an autonomous republic for Jewish farmers. A paradise compared to this mess, I can tell you. Except the winters were hellish. And now I am a zealous architect. I might just turn around and become a zealous socialist again. It is possible. I am related to that bastard Kaganovich, the last Jewish Stalinist until Khrushchev kicked him in the teeth.

UM HISHAM: My daughter, Asma, liked the turtles best.

SHLOMO: God, I'm hungry.

UM HISHAM: Of course you are. So buck up. There's a fresh ruin in the Salahaddin district of Rafah *(Breathes)* Can you smell the dust in the air?

SHLOMO *(Breathes, too)*: Yes. Yes I can smell it. The crumble of walls. The smell of crushed linen. Toys bursting like fruit beneath the 'dozer's blade. Where in Salahaddin?

UM HISHAM: Second street from the left, number five. There were pigeons on the roof. Six of them.

SHLOMO: How many rooms in the house?

UM HISHAM: Four rooms. Large ones.

SHLOMO: Delicious. Thank you.

(Shlomo exits excitedly.)

UM HISHAM: And the walls in the bathroom were blue. In the hall there were orange birds on the tiles on the floor.

YUVAL: Yes. Orange birds on the floor. That's my mother's house.

UM HISHAM: And the ceiling was yellow.

YUVAL: No. The ceiling in my mother's house is white. And on the wall the tiles are—

YUVAL AND UM HISHAM: blue flowers with pink leaves.

YUVAL: How do you know this? What the fuck are you saying? I know that hallway. I know it like the back of my hand.

UM HISHAM: Yes. You have beautiful hands. But do you know your own hands? What do they do while you sleep?

YUVAL *(Playful)*: Uh-oh. Are you getting nasty on me?

UM HISHAM: Weeks ago. Your forefinger pressed the starter on your brand-new Merkava tank.

YUVAL: Merkava. Baddest bad-assed tank to ever float the desert. Have you heard the stereo systems on those mother fuckers? It's like a concert you can hear from the moon.

(Yuval does some air guitar and screams out a couple lines of rock and roll, but just the tune, not words. Then he quits abruptly and stares at Um Hisham. Suddenly she does the rock and roll lines back to him, but even better. Then she stares back.)

UM HISHAM: And with five other tanks and two bulldozers you met the tortoises.

YUVAL: So this is about the damn turtles?

UM HISHAM: Yes. It begins with the turtles. In the zoo. The tiny zoo in Al-Brazil, Rafah. In Gaza. The turtles lined up to defend the zoo. They say their armor was aglow in the dusty light. That you could see it for miles. But your treads are four feet wide and the Merkava tank weighs sixty tons.

YUVAL: Sixty-five tons. Fully loaded. The new fire-control system developed by El Op includes advanced features with the capability to acquire and lock onto moving targets.

UM HISHAM: Turtles are moving targets.

YUVAL: The Merkava 4 is powered by a GD 883 V-12 diesel engine rated at fifteen hundred HP.

YUVAL AND UM HISHAM: The new engine represents a twenty-five-percent increase in power . . .

YUVAL: compared to the twelve-hundred HP power pack . . .

UM HISHAM: installed on the Merkava 3. Weight: sixty-five tons, fully loaded, as you say. A turtle weighs a kilo and a half. It was a quick death for the turtles. Then you and your buddies crushed the rest of the zoo. The ostrich was flattened, as were the squirrels, goats and kangaroos. The single deer lay on her side all night, paddling with her broken legs as though she were swimming.

YUVAL: Hey. The military dismissed those accusations.

UM HISHAM: Why the zoo? The only place for children to go to touch animals and hear their sounds.

YUVAL: I told you why. Because gurgling is no longer permitted. There was gurgling coming from the Rafah zoo, day in, day out. Gurgle, gurgle, gurgle. The children were gurgling.

UM HISHAM: Not gurgling. Singing.

YUVAL: Same thing.

UM HISHAM: No. It's not.

YUVAL: I'm not a bad soldier.

UM HISHAM: You never killed a human being. Though perhaps, sooner or later.

YUVAL: Plato said: "If there were only some way of contriving that a state or an army should be made up of lovers, they would be the very best governors of their own city."

UM HISHAM: Perhaps. But not of ours.

YUVAL: I'm sorry about the zoo.

UM HISHAM: You never wanted to be a soldier, Yuval.

YUVAL: Don't be ridiculous. If it weren't for the state of Israel, I would not exist.

UM HISHAM: Do you believe that, Yuval? Do your friends believe that?

YUVAL: Sometimes. Some of them. But then there are moments when I am putting my feet into clean socks or drinking cold water on a hot day and something falls somewhere in the house and breaks and it sounds almost beautiful and then I feel a sharp—what is it? —a burning. And I just don't know anymore.

UM HISHAM: Tell your mother, when you see her, that I have something that belongs to her.

YUVAL: Just give it to me. She won't meet with you. I'll see she gets it. There are regulations on what we can carry. How much does it weigh?

UM HISHAM: I don't know.

YUVAL: How big is it?

UM HISHAM: About three minutes.

YUVAL: That's not size, that's time.

UM HISHAM: And yet it is more precious to a mother than anything in the world.

YUVAL: Then give me the minutes that belong to my mother. Hey. If they belong to her, give them back. We stole your land, you stole our minutes. Now give them back.

(Shlomo enters flustered.)

SHLOMO: The soldiers wouldn't let me past to measure the new ruin. How the hell is an architect to get work when they won't let me inspect the property? *(To Yuval)* An IDF soldier has been killed there. They are investigating.

YUVAL: How did he die?

SHLOMO: A bullet from a Rafah sniper. In the head.

UM HISHAM: My daughter, Asma, was eleven years old. She was always counting.

YUVAL: Shit. A fellow soldier down. *(To Um Hishem)* You see, you people are murderers!

UM HISHAM: My husband and I used to tease her that she was born with a book in her head, a book of numbers. But this did not make her a sour child. On the contrary, Asma was always laughing and at the end of the day she'd say, "Mother, you have taken one thousand forty-four steps in the kitchen today." Or, "Father, you have pulled on your ear seventeen times this afternoon." And, "Look at me, I have made eighty-three circles in the air with my toe!" She had six pigeons. She named them One, Two, Three, Four, Five—

YUVAL AND SHLOMO: and Six.

UM HISHAM: No. After Five came Nine. Nine was a surprise. Like Asma, always a surprise. An Israeli bullet. To the chest. Except she was not carrying a gun. She was on the roof, tending her pigeons.

YUVAL: You're right. I never wanted to be a soldier.

SHLOMO: I fought for a splendid cause, in another age, another land. I miss it. I am lonely.

UM HISHAM: So you have said.

SHLOMO: Before we attacked I said to our colonel, Novikov was his name, I said, "I love you and I believe in you."

UM HISHAM: At Stalingrad?

YUVAL: Don't encourage him.

SHLOMO: And off we went and encircled the German 6th Army. Or maybe I read about it. I don't know anymore. But that "love and belief," it was so strong then—now, what of them? Torn apart, like the three of us.

YUVAL: I have nothing to do with you, or her.

SHLOMO: Ah, the love of my life.

UM HISHAM: Who?

SHLOMO: Stalingrad, and the thousands of Russian tanks roaring across the steppes, through the luminous snow. Liberation! But—

UM HISHAM: There is always a but.

SHLOMO: She turned out to be a bitch. Stabbed us in the back. Turned out to be Stalin in drag. And now, my precious sentiments?—"love and belief"—where are they? They have left a hole. That is why I am always hungry. But I cannot cry any longer. Too much dust in my eyes. See?

(Yuval picks up his gun, slings it over his shoulder.)

YUVAL: Get out of my zoo. Both of you. It's beginning to get dark. The noise will start, the roaring. Pieces of the animals will begin to fall off. You don't want to see it. Only a soldier's got the guts for this business. *(To Um Hisham)* I'm sorry about your daughter.

UM HISHAM: I don't want your sorry. I could not hold her. Bleeding among the feathers and bird shit. Was she afraid? Did she call out for me? As she lay on her back, dying, what did she count? The noises in the sky hanging over her? Or the beats of her draining heart? I know Asma, so I know she counted something. I can't sleep for thinking about it. But what? What do you think she counted?

YUVAL: I don't know.

UM HISHAM: Make a wild guess, Soldier.

YUVAL: Her breath.

UM HISHAM: Shut your mouth now.

YUVAL: Maybe she counted her breath. In and out. In and out.

UM HISHAM: In and out. Maybe. But I will never know. What I know is Asma died alone. *(In Arabic)* For this I will never forgive even God.

SHLOMO: Um Hisham. I, too, am sorry about your daughter. That was not a part of my architectural plan. Though sometimes we must build on top of it . . .

UM HISHAM: Leave us, Shlomo.

SHLOMO: I would like to stay a little while.

UM HISHAM: Not now. You have more work in Salahaddin. Your ruins are missing you.

SHLOMO: Yes, we see eye to eye, the ruins and I. *(Beat)* Yet all I see are ruins. Ah well, Homa Umigdal, Homa—

UM HISHAM: Go. You will come visit again tomorrow. I always expect you.

SHLOMO *(In Arabic)*: And I will always expect you, Um Hisham. Until tomorrow then. Let us go with God.

(Shlomo leaves.)

YUVAL: He speaks Arabic?

UM HISHAM: Of course he does. When you get that old all languages possess you. Now I must go, too. I'll be back tomorrow.

(Um Hisham puts on her head scarf again.)

YUVAL: Give your family my condolences. I mean that.

UM HISHAM: Yes. I believe you do. My condolences to your mother.

YUVAL: Why?

UM HISHAM: It's a terrible thing to lose a child.

YUVAL: My mother hasn't lost a child. How dare you?

UM HISHAM: Yuval.

YUVAL: Are you threatening my family? Are you fucking threatening my family?

UM HISHAM: I have thought of sending your mother a bouquet but I am too angry and I hate the smell of flowers. I think of your mother. I don't want to, but I do. We had pieces of life in common. In our children. Our children were our pieces of life. Now we have pieces of death. In common.

YUVAL: No.

UM HISHAM: I'm sorry.

YUVAL: No.

UM HISHAM: It's all right.

YUVAL: You're a liar! *(Beat)* I am alive, you hear me! I am alive. I am alive! *(Shouts)* I am alive!

(They both are silent a moment. Um Hisham speaks, just telling the story, not reliving it. Yuval listens quietly.)

UM HISHAM: You came to my house in Rafah at 5:30 A.M., with two other soldiers. You broke down the door. Your friends found no weapons in my house. How could they? We had none. Your friends were pissed-off so they began to beat my husband. He was on the ground. They kicked him in the chest seven times. If Asma had been there she would have counted. But then you stopped them. Why did you stop them?

(Yuval just looks at her.)

I was so grateful that I made you a cup of tea. And you accepted. You stood in the hallway, the dawn light from the broken door rushing past you. You put the cup to your lips. *(Beat)* A single bullet from a sniper. To the head. You went down on one knee, still holding the cup. You looked at me as though it were a joke—all of it—that moment, the tea spilling across your thighs, the orange birds on the tiled floor, my face so close to your face. You said—

YUVAL: Don't. I don't want to know what I said.

UM HISHAM: You said—

YUVAL: I don't want to know.

UM HISHAM: "Hold me." And you kept saying it.

YUVAL *(Quietly)*: Hold me. Hold me. Hold me.

UM HISHAM: Three minutes. It took you three minutes to die. Everything I have despised, for decades—the uniform, the power, the brutality, the inhumanity—and I held it in my arms. I held you, Yuval. *(Beat)* But it should have been your mother. We should hold our own children when they die.

(After some moments:)

YUVAL: Then I am in hell.

UM HISHAM: No, Yuval. You are in the Rafah zoo. The one that still lives in our minds. And every day I'll come here and visit you, as I visit my daughter.

YUVAL: They bulldozed your house because I died there.

UM HISHAM: Yes.

YUVAL: They arrested your husband.

UM HISHAM: Yes.

YUVAL: You come here every day, don't you?

UM HISHAM: I have no choice.

YUVAL: Plato said: "He whom love touches not, walks in darkness." It's not dark here. Not always. Does that mean I walk in love?

UM HISHAM: I hope so. For your sake.

YUVAL: All right. *(Beat)* Well, I need to go feed the porcupine. We've become pretty close, as close as a soldier and a porcupine can get. Wait. That song you were singing earlier. I know it. How fucking ironic, huh, that I'd heard it before. You sang it as I died.

UM HISHAM: Yes.

YUVAL: Please. Sing it for me. Again.

UM HISHAM: No.

(Um Hisham starts to leave. Yuval goes back to his zookeeping. But then Um Hisham begins to sing the same song she sang at the beginning of the play, the song she sang as Yuval died. Her back is to Yuval as she sings. Yuval, his back also to Um Hisham, hears the song and becomes still, listening. Then Yuval slowly turns his head as though the song is calling to him from some long distance. Then one of his knees gives way and he slowly sinks to the ground. He lies on his back, still. Um Hisham finishes her song. Then she turns her head and stares at the dead Yuval. In this fleeting gesture/moment, they connect. Blackout.)

END OF VISION ONE

Vision Two

Between This Breath and You

CHARACTERS

MOURID KAMAL	Palestinian, a father, forties
TANYA LANGER	Israeli, twenty years old
SAMI ELBAZ	Israeli, Moroccan descent, early thirties

PLACE

A clinic waiting room in West Jerusalem. Very bare, a few chairs. Not "realistic."

TIME

The present.

NOTE

Between Vision One and Two, there should be unexpected music or sound.

A bare waiting room in a medical clinic. A row of five to six simple, hard chairs. Mourid is sitting completely still, hands on his knees, waiting, assured. For someone, something. Sami, wearing a baseball cap, enters with his mop, sees Mourid.

SAMI: We're closed. Okay? Closed. You don't speak English, eh?

(Sami begins to methodically stack the chairs until constructing a mini wall between himself and Mourid. He looks over the chairs at Mourid. Mourid ignores him. Sami then uses his string mop as a puppet: the mop "peeks" over the chairs at Mourid.)

SAMI/MOP: It's late. We're it's. Closed. Late. We're tits. Clothes. Latte. We're nits. Clogs. Lattice. Waffle house pits. Latex. Werewolves and gits.

(Mourid continues to sit and stare out front. Sami lowers the mop and begins to mop.

SAMI *(Energetically)*: Ever been to the Dead Sea? No? No. Well, it's not the salt that makes you float but the shit, shit, shit. Excrement, an excellent floating device.

When you are a kid, you can pick up a shell and hear the sea in your ear. Today, day in day out, I hear the sea, my mop and the shit. It rings. No. It hisses, shushes, sighs in my ears like some alien lullaby.

(Sami rests on his mop.)

SSSSSSSHHHHHHHUUUSSHHHHHHH! I'm the ancient mariner: water, water, everywhere, and not a drop to drink because it comes from assholes, toilets and sinks!
MOURID: A poet as well.
SAMI: Shit.
MOURID: Your favorite subject.
SAMI: I didn't realize you could speak. English.
MOURID: And make sense of it, too. But please, don't let me interrupt you.
SAMI: Of course not.

(Sami continues, but not directly to Mourid:)

When they ask me, though they never ask me, but when they ask me, "If you could be reborn what would you be? An eel? An isopod? A tuna?" They would limit the choices to fish because they know I'm a mariner of sorts and envy fish. Still I would surprise them because I'd say— Are you listening, man?— I'd say, "I want to be reborn as a. Mop." Yes. A mop. Not a synthetic one, of course. But one of these old-fashioned ones of wool and cotton; stick made of hardwood, fresh from a tree. I'd spend my life as a mop in the arms of an earnest cleaner, licking up the refuse from the linoleum, the slate, the marble. And you know why? Huh? Because there is no surface in the world more intimate than a human floor. We leave everything behind on it: our hair, our skin, our drippings and droolings, our lint, our nefarious discards, our shameful discords. With what this mop gathers I could build, particle by particle, out of abandoned parts, an entirely new human being! A mop is an extension of Divine power, a gatherer of the slough; a mop is, in short, a functional God. And you are obstructing my God. It's after hours. The nurse will see you tomorrow.

MOURID: Thank you. The nurse will see me today.

SAMI: Where did you learn your English?

MOURID: Imperial College. London. Engineering.

SAMI: Bah. Imperial College. Me, I'm a self-made man. Both English and biology. Just me and my books. Then I did graduate studies at Hebrew University.

MOURID: You are a liar.

SAMI: In this instance, yes. Hebrew University rejected me.

MOURID: I must see the nurse.

SAMI: And I must finish mopping before I can go home.

MOURID: Tell the nurse that Mourid is waiting for her.

(Sami looks closely at Mourid for the first time.)

SAMI: Oh. My. God. You're her lover! Tanya has a West Bank lover!

MOURID: I am not her lover.

SAMI *(Speaks to his mop)*: You little fool, Tanya! How could you fall for one of them! Don't you know they are the

29

worst sort of. Higplenoffenmopsters! *(Shakes the mop)* Snap out of it! Snap out of it, girl! Find a decent man *(Beat)* like me!

MOURID: Tanya. So that's her first name. Tanya.

SAMI: After you had ravished her, not even the decency to ask her name?

MOURID: I am a married man.

SAMI: Adulterer!

MOURID: Though my wife is dead. Two years now.

SAMI: Cheating on a dead wife!

MOURID *(Matter of fact)*: There is something wrong with you.

SAMI: That's what Hebrew University said. And I said: "Do you really think I resemble an insect?" No . . .

MOURID: Tanya has something that belongs to me.

SAMI: . . . then why did the authorities spray my father with DDT when he entered Tel Aviv?

MOURID: All Arabs are filthy?

SAMI: But I am a Jewish Arab.

MOURID: Yes. I can tell by the mop.

SAMI: And you have nothing but a dead wife. That's why you want my Tanya!

MOURID: Your Tanya?

SAMI: She doesn't realize yet that she is mine.

MOURID: Finish your job. Go home. Make a child.

SAMI: I am alone. Does it show? I mop from clinic to clinic. I haven't kissed a woman in years. Does she not have a beautiful name, Tanya? She loves New York. Tanya.

MOURID: Yes.

MOURID AND SAMI: Tanya . . .

(Tanya appears. She is a calm, direct young woman. Mourid stands up. Tanya does not acknowledge him.)

TANYA *(In Hebrew)*: Sami? Is that your name? You realize we are closed?

SAMI: Yes, Miss Langer. But English please. I must practice for my future.

TANYA: Sami Telbaz?

SAMI: Sami Elbaz. The replacement mopper since the first of last month.

TANYA: Have you told this gentleman that we closed two hours ago? He'll have to go to the public clinic or come back tomorrow.

SAMI: Yes, I did tell him. But he won't budge. Said he had to see you . . . Tanya.

(This is the first time Sami has called Tanya by her first name. Tanya studies Sami.)

TANYA: It's Miss Langer.

SAMI: Miss Langer. *(Beat)* I could whack him with my mop.

TANYA: No, Sami. I'll take care of it.

SAMI: Yes, Miss Langer. Miss Langer . . . Tanya.

TANYA: Sami!

SAMI: Tanya!

TANYA: Go finish up in the office. Then go home.

(Sami gives Mourid a dirty look, then exits slowly, dragging his mop behind him. Tanya looks for the first time at Mourid. She waits.)

MOURID: Miss Langer. It is a blessing to meet you.

(Mourid holds out his hand, but Tanya does not take it.)

TANYA: I've been on my feet ten hours. I can give you five minutes, no more. What is the problem?

MOURID: There are many problems, Miss Langer.
TANYA: Is it a problem with appetite?

(Mourid shakes his head no.)

How is your sleep?
MOURID: My sleep is very well, thank you for asking. I haven't seen it in years but I hear it's thriving.
TANYA: Let's have a look in your eyes.

(Tanya signals for Mourid to take a seat. She shines a light in his eyes.)

How's your sight?
MOURID: Belligerent. I focus on the road, it wanders with the goats.
TANYA: Is your vision clear?
MOURID: Yes. May God curse it.
TANYA: Look, do you need a prescription?
MOURID: I have never been to New York. I hear the subways are ugly. The parks beautiful. At night, Manhattan glows like a gigantic firefly.

(After a moment:)

TANYA: I see. So this is not actually a medical problem.
      I could call the police. How did you get in here?
MOURID: Where is "here"? *(Beat)* This clinic?
TANYA: West Jerusalem.
MOURID: I walked.
TANYA: You can't walk through the Wall.
MOURID: There are always cracks.
TANYA: Good night. And get out.

(Mourid stands.)

MOURID: I am truly unwell, Miss Langer. You can help me.

TANYA: This is a private clinic. You'll have to pay.

MOURID: I have no money. Don't turn me away, please. You are a nurse.

(After a moment:)

TANYA: What exactly is the problem?

(Mourid sits again.)

MOURID: I am stuck.

TANYA: Your bowels? How are your bowels?

MOURID: My bowels are pleasant. My bowels are actually very much like the English: punctual, polite, predictable. Abroad they are murderous, especially in slippers.

TANYA: Have you been here before?

MOURID: No.

TANYA: I recognize your voice.

MOURID: We've never spoken.

TANYA: If I am to help you, we must be direct.

MOURID: In my ears I hear a rushing.

(Tanya looks into his ears.)

TANYA: A "rushing"?

MOURID: Wind through a pipe. Did you know, Tanya—may I call you Tanya?—that wind has no sound? What makes the sound are the things it touches—branch, cliff, roof. All that rushing is the contact between one thing and another. Without that meeting point between two worlds, the harshest wind is silent.

TANYA: Your ears are fine.

MOURID: My throat hurts.

TANYA: Open your mouth.

(Tanya looks into his mouth.)

Your throat looks okay.

MOURID: It's always dry.

TANYA: That happens when we age.

MOURID: I once dreamed water could be the solution. But you've closed the tap. Your lawns are so green they are blue. I can hear you splashing in your swimming pools in my sleep.

TANYA: You are suffering from depression. I'll suggest a prescription to the doctor. Seroxat. Full strength. You'll have to come back and collect it tomorrow.

(Tanya takes out a small notebook.)

How do you spell your name?

MOURID: Mourid Kamal. K.A.M.A.L. Will pills clear up my depression?

TANYA *(Smiles)*: Yes. They will.

MOURID: Thank you, Tanya.

TANYA: You're welcome.

MOURID: But I want to keep my depression.

TANYA: Depression is a disease, Mr. Kamal.

MOURID: No. Depression is a warning. Cystic fibrosis is a disease.

TANYA: Cystic fibrosis?

MOURID: Yes. It eats the lungs. Termites into wood. Rust into steel. Until the lungs collapse into a pile of rotting pus and

follicles and steamed bronchioles and wilted bronchi.
And the dying alveoli are not tasteful either.

TANYA: I'm sorry. I can't help you with that.

MOURID: My son's name is Ahmed.

TANYA: For a condition that serious, you'll have to go to the hospital for treatment.

MOURID: He's not much younger than you, a few years. His big toe on his left foot is slightly irregular. Do you think, Tanya, that one can build a boy out of a single toe? Sometimes I build him from his eyebrows, spreading out over his forehead. Please. Take my pulse. I have a fear of death.

TANYA *(Takes his pulse)*: We all must die. One of these days.

MOURID: I have a terror I will never die.

TANYA: You have a good heaven in store for you, Mr. Kamal.

MOURID: Yes. I believe in Allah, praise be to God. But what is a good heaven? Will there be gulls, or just the trace of them? Good coffee or just the aroma? Will there be sex or just the smell of it?

TANYA *(Listening to his chest)*: Breathe in deep, let it out slowly.

(Mourid does as she asks.)

Again.

(Mourid does.)

You're lungs are sound. Who diagnosed you with cystic fibrosis?

MOURID: Who diagnosed you?

TANYA *(After a moment, firmly)*: I don't have cystic fibrosis. Your five minutes is up.

MOURID: Were you born in New York City?

TANYA: No. I was born in Tel Aviv. I went to boarding school in Boston. It's my responsibility to lock up, so if you won't leave, I'll have to call security. You'll spend the week in jail.

MOURID: Please keep your kindness in check.

TANYA: At the very least.

MOURID: Boarding school abroad. Flights home for Hanukkah and school holidays. Ahmed went to school in a building that was made of two sticks and a stone.

TANYA: I don't do sentimentality, Mr. Kamal.

MOURID: That's too bad. My sentimentality has no limits.

TANYA: We don't go easy on trespassers.

MOURID: Do you think this is the only world? I can hear conversations happening one hundred years ago. The things my son said. The words you will say, after your death.

TANYA *(Even)*: Are you threatening me?

MOURID: I want to touch you.

TANYA: Shame on you. Act your age. In my clinic, you'll have some respect.

MOURID: You are not a nurse, Tanya. You are a nurse's aid.

TANYA: How could you know that?

MOURID: You're not qualified to make a diagnosis.

TANYA: I will qualify for a full nursing degree in eighteen months.

MOURID: How often do you stay behind to lock up? To play with the stethoscope? To talk with a patient after hours, pretending you can be of service? Yes. Let's call security. I have some things to tell them.

TANYA: Your word means nothing against mine. You know that.

MOURID: That is true. But I can put a little bug in someone's ear. It wouldn't look good for you, Tanya. Trust is key in your profession. Between you and your patients. Between you and your colleagues.

TANYA: What do you want from me?

MOURID: Just to talk a little while. Together in this room.

TANYA: Do you want to hurt me?

MOURID: No. I do not want to hurt you. I want to tell you about my son. When he was twelve the IDF gave him a broom. They made him sweep the dirt from their tanks. The children had been throwing dirt.

TANYA: How innocent.

MOURID: The back of the head and pelvis. Your soldiers shot him twice.

TANYA: Why?

MOURID: They said he was carrying a gun.

TANYA: Was he?

MOURID: No.

(Tanya stares at Mourid for some moments.)

TANYA: I am sorry for your loss, Mr. Kamal.

MOURID: Sometimes a death is more than a loss. It's an abyss. A quiet howling. Can you hear that howling? Listen.

(He listens. Tanya takes some tablets from her uniform.)

TANYA: Here. These should you help with that noise.

MOURID: You're not qualified to hand out a prescription.

TANYA: No, I'm not.

(Tanya puts the tablets in Mourid's shirt pocket.)

MOURID: Thank you.

TANYA: It's normal to grieve for years after the violent death of a loved one.

MOURID: But, Tanya, there was a bottom to that abyss. A miracle. My son did not die.

TANYA: That is a miracle. But a bullet in the back of his head? Is he not. Well, I mean, his brain, is he—

MOURID: The bullet carved out half his brain.

TANYA: I see.

MOURID: Yes. I see, also. And I sometimes still feel it on my hands, lumpy and warm like a hearty porridge. Imagine the shame of entertaining such a metaphor as your child dies in your arms.

TANYA: But you said he lived.

MOURID: Tanya.

(Mourid nears Tanya. She holds her ground. He raises his arm and at first it is not clear what he will do. Then he puts his hand on her breast. For a moment, neither of them moves. Then Tanya slaps Mourid. He withdraws his hand from her chest.)

You caught your breath when I touched you. I felt you. Catch your breath. What a strange phrase: "to catch one's breath." As though it wished to escape our grasp forever.

TANYA *(Calmly)*: I realize you are grieved. Perhaps even temporarily—

MOURID: Insane.

TANYA: Whatever happened to your son, be he dead or a singing vegetable, you will not touch my breasts.

MOURID: I don't want to touch your breasts.

TANYA *(Calls loudly, keeping her eyes on Mourid)*: Sami!

(Sami appears with his mop.)

SAMI: Tanya.

TANYA: Call the police.

SAMI *(Brandishing his mop)*: Let me take him. He looks slow.

TANYA: No. Call the police.

SAMI: But it could look bad if you know him.

TANYA: Before tonight, I had no connection to him whatsoever.

MOURID: That's not true. We are unbearably intimate.

TANYA: I'll call the police myself.

(Tanya turns to go.)

MOURID *(Speaking rapidly)*: If you do that, Tanya, you will never know how I know you often wake in the night, and you are falling and clawing at your face trying to dislodge something caught in your mouth and you cannot breathe.

SAMI: Okay. Time for the cops.

TANYA: Wait, Sami. Stay. *(To Mourid)* Your cheap tricks do not impress me, Mr. Kamal: everyone dreams of suffocation.

MOURID: Not that often.

TANYA: Who are you?

SAMI: He's a widow. He's looking for a new wife. Isn't it obvious? But what has he got to offer, huh? Three olive pits and a hand shake? Exactly. *(To Mourid)* How 'bout a cup of water? *(To Tanya)* Has he even offered you a cup of water?

MOURID: Tanya knows that water is no longer a part of my life.

SAMI: Then you have nothing. And now I'm going to pull the ground right out from under you! *(Beat)* Oh. Forgive me. An unfortunate metaphor for a West Banker. But never mind. Tanya. Allow me to compete with this suitor. I have two strong mopping arms, strapping arms, stropping mops. I speak Hebrew, Arabic, English—and Biology, fluently. I am a mariner.

He was shrewd adventurer, tough and hardy
By many a tempest had his beard been shaken.
And he knew all the harbors that there were
Between the Baltic and Cape Finisterre.

Chaucer.

If I could find a sturdy boat
I'd unfurl, and float and float.

That's me. Gifts? Two mops, one bucket and three kinds
of desire: hot, cold, and Oh My God.

(Tanya looks at both men and shakes her head in disbelief.)

MOURID: I'm sorry that I touched you, Miss Langer. I could
not help myself. I won't touch you again. Give me just a
few more minutes. After today I will not return unless you
request it. Please.
SAMI: Yes. Could not help the minutes today. Just a few more
selves I'm sorry for. After the touch could not help.
Request you unless it, please.

(For the first time Tanya really looks at Sami. She listens.)

Yes. Touching you. Mopping me. Topping him: the bastard. Because I have the gift of knowledge. Though I can't
practice it here. I would like a professorship and I've been
given a mop. But I specialize in isopods. Did you know
that I am deeply familiar with one of the world's most
sophisticated isopods, including wood lice? *Cymothoa
exigua. (To Mourid and Tanya)* Say it!
MOURID AND TANYA: *Cymothoa exigua.*

SAMI: That's right. This tiny isopod chooses the mouth of the spotted rose snapper fish for its home. It latches onto the fish's tongue with its little hooked legs and gradually eats away the fish's tongue. Then it grips tightly, oh so tightly, to the stub and effectively becomes the fish's tongue, growing as its host grows and feeding on bits of meat that float free as the fish eats. Speaking of unbearable intimacy. For all we know, any of us could have had our tongues devoured while we slept, and in the morning, a creature has latched onto our stubs, masquerading as our tongues, and we don't know it. Will it talk in a way that deceives us? Will it grow from the garbage that floats free as we speak?

(Tanya continues to stare at Sami for some moments. He smiles broadly at her, thinking he has won her over. Mourid steps in front of Sami.)

MOURID: Miss Langer. I had meant for our first meeting to unfold quite differently.

TANYA *(To Mourid)*: I don't understand you. Do you want to know if I am single? Yes. I am. Again and again, I'm single.

MOURID: But why? You are intelligent—

SAMI: Beautiful—

TANYA: Don't. I had a fiancé. He left. Like the one before him. At present I'm not interested in anything long term. What was your son's name?

MOURID: Ahmed. If he had grown up, if we lived in a different hour, you might have fallen in love with him. Shall I build him for you? I will begin with the left shoulder. On its blade he had a mole. He—

TANYA: No, Mr. Kamal. Don't build him for me.

MOURID: Only for you.

SAMI: Then let me build him. For both of you!

(Sami stands his mop upright. He is serious and careful in this demonstration.)

About this tall?

MOURID: You're not qualified to build Ahmed. You never met him.

SAMI: This tall?

(After a moment's hesitation:)

MOURID: A little shorter.

(Sami carefully adjusts the height, until it's right.)

No. No. No. Yes. That's right.

TANYA: This is ridiculous.

(Sami fluffs the "hair" of the mop.)

MOURID: He had thick hair, yes, like that. But not hanging in his face.

(Sami adjusts the "hair" away from the "face"; he is taking this exercise seriously.)

Yes. Exactly. I'm beginning to see him now.

SAMI: Ahmed.

MOURID: Yes, my Ahmed.

TANYA: I see nothing.

SAMI: Did he wear a hat?

MOURID: No, no. *(Beat)* Actually, yes. When he was six or seven he wore a red baseball cap. He used it as a basket to collect interesting pebbles, when it wasn't on his head. Please, go on.

(Sami whips off his cap and puts it on the mop.)

Hmmm. Maybe. Maybe. A certain likeness.

(Sami stands the mop to attention, between himself and Mourid, so its the three of them, together.)

Can you see him now, Tanya? The moment of him. The flash.

TANYA: No.

MOURID: The idea.

SAMI: But you are not really looking, Miss Langer.

MOURID: The color.

TANYA: No.

MOURID: We are here, Tanya.

SAMI: Yes. We. are. here.

TANYA: Sami.

SAMI: Yes, Miss Langer.

TANYA: You're fired.

SAMI: Up. Up. Yes. I am Fired. Up. Because I can build a human being, but here I cannot build a life.

(Sami takes the cap off the mop, puts it on his own head, then lowers the mop to be a "mop" again.)

I can't even float on the shit of the Dead Sea because I am terrified of water. Imagine, a biologist who is afraid of water. Fired? Fired? I fire you, too, Tanya Langer. For your inability to see the boy in a mop or the mop in every human being. Nevertheless, let me help you. Don't move. Please.

(Sami "mops" Mourid's body. Mourid does not move. Then he "mops" Tanya's body. She also remains still.)

There. You are both blessed by my instrument of God. Sail well. Sail safe. Good-bye. Good-bye. But watch your tongues. Watch your tongues!

(Sami exits with his mop.)

TANYA: I feel sad for your loss, Mr. Kamal. But tonight will come and tonight will pass. And I am already forgetting your sorrow.

(Tanya moves to leave.)

MOURID: You will not become a full-fledged nurse, Tanya. In eighteen months you will be dead.

TANYA: How dare you.

MOURID: Though you have envied your superiors' medical uniforms, you will never wear one.

TANYA: Wrong. I stole one from the laundry room months ago. I sleep in it at night. In my dreams I qualify to do anything.

MOURID: I never had cystic fibrosis. You did.

TANYA: So that's what you want? Will you leave me alone then if I admit it? Yes. I had cystic fibrosis. In the end I could not breathe.

MOURID: Now you can breathe.

TANYA: Double lung transplant. October 17th. Five years ago.

MOURID: Today.

TANYA: Yes. Five years ago today.
MOURID: The day after Ahmed died.

(Tanya considers the implication, but only for a second.)

TANYA: My donor was a young Jewish student from Haifa.
MOURID: You were still a child then. Like Ahmed.
TANYA: My donor died in an automobile accident.
MOURID: The donor organs had to be transplanted within six hours after being removed. While you were under general anesthesia, the surgeon made an incision across your chest, beneath the breast area and removed your lungs. Then the surgeon placed the new lungs into your empty chest cavity and connected the pulmonary artery of the new lungs into your vessels and airway. Drainage tubes were inserted to drain air, fluid and blood out of your chest for several days to allow the lungs to reexpand. With oxygen. Sweet, cold oxygen. And here you are, beautiful Tanya. *(Beat)* My son is inside you.

(After a moment:)

TANYA: You are a grieving, pathetic, gibbering lunatic. Her name, my donor's name, was Amira Goldensohn.
MOURID: Ahmed is inside you.

(Tanya is silent. Then she begins to laugh. She laughs and laughs.)

It is beautiful to hear you laugh. It takes more air to laugh than to speak. When you inhale, my son's lungs extract the oxygen from the air, then distribute it via the bloodstream to every cell in your body.

(Tanya stops laughing.)

TANYA: You are wrong, Mr. Kamal.

MOURID: I am certain.

TANYA: You can prove nothing.

MOURID: I can speak to my son.

TANYA: You are out of your mind.

MOURID: I am a father. A father can speak to his son no matter the circumstances. You cannot prevent it.

TANYA: You can speak to your son? What? Use my ear as a telephone? Like this? *(She speaks into Mourid's ear)* Hello? Hello, Ahmed? This is your father speaking. How's the weather in there?

(Tanya spits on Mourid.)

Oh my. It's raining.

(Mourid moves away and wipes his ear with a handkerchief.)

MOURID: You are one tough nut.

TANYA: Good-bye, Mr. Kamal. It's been a real adventure. But it's time for you to seek out another sucker. I won't be yours. I bet you've accosted half a dozen transplant patients, telling each one that he or she is filled to the gills with your son. I'm still young, Mr. Kamal. I know I won't have the time to ravish this cold world the way I'd like to. But I do know this: unlike most transplant patients who experience at least one episode of organ rejection, my body did not reject the donor lungs.

MOURID: I am so grateful.

TANYA: Had your son's lungs been inside me, I am sure, absolutely sure, that I would have rejected them.

MOURID: There is no science to what you say. My son's lungs and your entire system proved compatible. That is a fact, a piece of luck, and a wonder. No one would tell me anything about you. To finally find you, after years of searching, to stand close enough to feel your breath, his breath . . . is a miracle. Ahmed's lungs were not taken from us. We gave them. Let us celebrate with a passionate tune my son liked to sing in the mornings before school.

(He sings with gusto:)

> She take my money.
> Well I'm in need.
> Yeah she's a triflin' friend indeed.
> Oh she's a gold digger,
> Way over town.
> That digs in me!

Kanye West. Brilliant. But my son liked the classics as well. This was his favorite oldie.

(He sings the opening lyrics of "Every Breath You Take.")

TANYA: The Police.
MOURID: Dreadful. Do you think he might have known he would die? Do you think he could have been practicing that song, for you?
TANYA: Mr. Kamal, I say: good night.

(Tanya moves to leave. With one hand, Mourid suddenly grabs Tanya's uniform from the back to keep her from leaving.)

MOURID: Ahmed, this is your father speaking to you: greetings. *(In Arabic, but not directly to Tanya)* How are you?

TANYA: Let go of me.

MOURID *(In Arabic)*: Praise be to God. I have missed you so much. I have so many things to say.

TANYA: Let go!

(Tanya firmly tries to shake Mourid off but he tightens his grip.)

MOURID: It has been too long, Ahmed. But Tanya must not leave me yet. Show her that you are my son. Show her.

(Tanya pulls free.)

TANYA: Whatever is inside me, you son of a bitch, it belongs to me now.

MOURID: Show her, Ahmed!

TANYA: You have no command over me. I am—

(Suddenly Tanya cannot breathe fully. She does not panic. She is controlled and contains her fear. She tries to breathe deeply but her breath is constricted. She takes short, tight breaths.)

MOURID: Now do you believe me, Tanya? Now do you know on whom you depend to breathe?

TANYA: This will pass . . . This will pass . . .

MOURID: Now do you believe me?

TANYA: I . . . I . . .

MOURID: That's enough, Ahmed.

(After a few moments, Tanya catches her breath. She can breathe evenly again.)

TANYA: Do you know, Mr. Kamal—

MOURID: Mourid. Please call me Mourid.

TANYA: Do you know, Mourid, why my fiancé left me? When I told him about the transplant, he said he couldn't bare to make the investment. The average life span of a lung transplantee is six years. I'd done nearly five when I met him.

MOURID: There is a woman in Canada who has lived more than twelve years. It's possible that with good care—

TANYA: Half of all patients die within five years after transplant, from infection and chronic rejection. I will probably die because of the toxic effects of the immunosuppressant medicines. It's extremely common.

MOURID: My son was in good health.

TANYA: In these last few months, at times, without warning, I have difficulty breathing. Sometimes, as you witnessed just now, when I am under pressure, for a few moments I lose my capacity altogether. But then it returns. It hardly frightens me anymore.

MOURID: There are techniques of breathing that can relax the transplanted lungs, allow for strengthening, perhaps allow for a few more years of life.

TANYA: There is nothing I haven't tried.

MOURID: But you haven't tried this with me, Tanya. I can teach you these techniques. You might still become a nurse!

TANYA: Let's say that for a moment, just a moment, that I accept the preposterous notion that my donor was your son—

MOURID: Ahmed. Please. His name was Ahmed.

TANYA: Then it would be true that I carry with me a piece of. Ahmed. Your son. You like that idea: a piece of Ahmed inside me.

(Mourid nods yes.)

In fact I'd say you are intoxicated with the idea, that it gives your entire being a shape and focus you would not have otherwise. Otherwise, you'd be just a bag of liquid grief— we could pick you up, poke a hole in the bottom, and you'd just spill away. But imagine the implications here—your son inside me—somehow alive inside me.

(She sings the rest of the refrain from "Every Breath You Take," picking up where Mourid left off.)

That would mean he accompanies me. Participates with me. Enjoys with me.

MOURID: Yes!

TANYA: When I laugh, your son laughs. When I sing, your son sings.

(Mourid joyously sings the song. Then they sing it together with vigor.)

But that would also mean your son was present last night. That's why I am especially tired today. I was awake till four A.M. I picked a stranger up after work. A sweet, eager young man. He fucked me so hard I thought he'd break me in half.

MOURID: How dare you—

TANYA: Don't worry. Things went smoothly. Your son gave me good air when I sucked cock. Good Jewish cock.

MOURID: No!

TANYA: And let me tell you, I do the deep-throat thing and I need all the oxygen I can get.

MOURID: Stop it! You must stop this ugliness!

TANYA: To cut it short: when I fuck an Israeli, your son fucks an Israeli. And when I have a good orgasm, your son—

(Mourid cries out. He rushes at Tanya threateningly, as though to hurt her. Tanya holds her ground. But then Mourid stops himself, and turns away. He takes a few steps as if to leave.)

And that's not all I do, Mr Kamal.

(Mourid stops, listening to her with his back.)

I don't have a steady boyfriend now. Vigorous activity tires me a little more each day. My family, they pretend I'm well. Denial is their elixir. "Tanya will outlive us all," my father says. I visit with them less and less. On my break here at work, I usually go to the park. I close my eyes and sit very still until I am no longer there, just the breathing. Just the breathing. And all the world is condensed into the fuel of oxygen, sliding in and out of my chest like the hands of God, working me, working my clay into a form that has no material existence, but is as solid and as palpable as this flesh. What is a good heaven? Yes. I'm afraid. But I imagine it to be a place of floating, where breathing is a continuous, circular motion, unchecked by the dependencies of this world. *(Beat)* That space where exhalation ends, before the next breath begins. That's where I want to— Where I want to— What is the dream I keep having, of falling and suffocation? How do you know about my dreams?

MOURID *(His back still to her)*: When Ahmed was five he fell down a well. He surfaced, roaring like a bull. He almost drowned. He used to dream that dream for years. He would wake bellowing.

TANYA: In the dream I am drowning but then two big arms lift me out of the water.

MOURID: I found my son just in time.

(Tanya stands very still. Her breathing has again become difficult, constricted. She takes short breaths and tries to smooth her breathing.)

You musn't fight the constriction. You must welcome it. Welcome it and it will pass. The short breaths you take are rigid and only make it worse.

(Only now does Mourid turn around.)

You must slow your breath down. Let it gather its force again. Like this.

(Mourid breathes in a long, slow breath.)

As though the air has become fluid and you are drinking it in.

(Mourid breathes in again, demonstrating.)

TANYA: I can't. *(Beat)* I can't.
MOURID: You must listen to me. You must follow my breath.
TANYA: Why do you want to help me?
MOURID: Because your name is Tanya Langer.

(Tanya shakes her head no.)

Because this is not the only world.

(Mourid and Tanya now face off, a good distance between them. It seems they are now in a different dimen-

sion, speaking to each other across a divide. They speak to one another slowly, formally:)

TANYA: Mourid Kamal. Why do you want to help me?
MOURID: Because you are. My son.

(Tanya looks at Mourid. Mourid raises his head slightly; Tanya copies him. It is clear that he is leading this breathing lesson. Mourid raises his hand slightly as though conducting their breaths. Together they begin a slow inhalation. Then an exhalation. The sound of their second inhalation is even deeper and seems to come from all around them. Before this second inhalation reaches its peak, the lights go black, and there is silence.)

END OF VISION TWO

Vision Three

The Retreating World

Ali enters, balancing a book on his head. He is dressed casually but carefully, in slacks and a button-down shirt.

ALI: Nowadays you can pick up a book like this for next to nothing. Whole libraries, years and years of careful selection and loving looks, and maybe some reading, set out by the side of the road. For sale. For next to nothing. Unfortunately I bought this one before. Before. And it cost me. But it was worth it.

(He tilts his head and lets the book drop to the floor.)

Books can be used for many things besides reading. *(Gives the book a couple of short, quick kicks)* For exercising the ankles and toes with short, controlled bursts of movement. Or *(Snatches up the book)* a book can be used to create a man with a bookish face. It can be done. *(Holds the book to hide his face for a moment)*

I never had the knack for telling good jokes. The kind that slap your face and send your head spinning. My friend Samir Saboura, he could tell jokes. Once he told me a joke about rice pudding, two porcupines and a jockstrap; I laughed so hard I broke a tooth.

But this, this is a book on bird "fancying" as they say in the north of England. It took me ages to understand, even though I am fluent in English and have read Macaulay's speeches in order to really hear the English language. But this was not English. This was north of English and about pigeons and doves. Not stuff for the faint-hearted.

It is a deadly serious book. One suspects, after fifty pages or so, that in fact it is not a book about keeping birds as a hobby, but something far more . . . important. Like how to keep your lover, or swindle your friends. Or find inner peace.

But after one has negotiated, appreciated and ingested the ins and outs of keeping pigeons, there are, considering the times—and you know what times we live in— whole libraries for sale, art books, leather bound in Baghdad in the thirties, obstetrics and radiology texts, copies of British medical journals. And something for you as well: first and second editions of *The Sun Also Rises*. *Waiting for Godot*. And all for the price of a few cigarettes. Considering the times there is only one real rule to keeping pigeons. And this rule, this golden rule, is *not* in this book—never name a pigeon after a member of your family or a dear friend. *(Beat)* For two reasons: pigeons have short lives—and when a pigeon named after an uncle dies, this can be disconcerting. And second: these times are dangerous for pigeons—they can be caught and eaten . . .

And cannibalism can put you off a hobby.

I began collecting and trading pigeons and doves when I was fifteen. That was more than ten years ago, when birds clustered like flies in the palms along the avenues, and my land was the land of dates. Do you remember that country? Back then, everyone could read and when my smallest dove developed a fever, I took her to the hospital, where there was free access to all health-care facilities. Parents were fined for not sending their pigeons to school. The basic indicators that you use to measure the overall well-being of flying animals were some of the best in the world. And. And. —Shut up, Ali. —One of the birds I called Lak'aa Faseeh Zayer, after my grandmother. A real show-off she was. This bird, known as the Dresden Trumpeter, I bought off a trader from North America: *Columba livia*, in Latin. It has a freestanding shell crest and a white wing shield. Now my grandmother was tall and hard as a big stick and she liked everything American. She drank her coffee from a Campbell's soup can. She worked as a maid in a hotel, wearing a set of trainers from a Sears Roebuck catalog a cousin sent her from Wisconsin. I was already a teenager when I got my first pigeon, but when I had trouble sleeping she would hold me in her arms and sing to me. Her voice was like an old soft motor, clinking and clanking. Much sweeter than any fruit.

(He sings a short Arab lullaby his grandmother taught him.)

She had only three teeth in front but she always said song was not in the tooth but in the roof of the mouth, where God lives. She was also a bit of a blasphemer. Lak'aa Faseeh Zayer was her name. I would write her name down for you but we have no pencils.

I became a student when I was seventeen. I had six birds by then. I had one white-winged dove, also imported from America. She I named Greta, after my little sister. My father he loved movies, and so my mother named my sister Greta, after Garbo. We were secular, our family. My birds, they were a mix of Christian, Jewish and Muslim. They pulled out each other's feathers when they got a chance, sometimes even a little blood, but mostly they got along well and crapped in the same pile. I won third prize with Greta in 1989 at the International Bird Show in Baghdad.

Books have other uses. *(Stands on the book)* Now I am an inch and a half taller. *(Stands with one foot off and one foot on)* Now I am a crooked man, a slanted man. Or to cut it short, for most of the world: an Arab. And I have come here to speak to you about pigeons.

My favorite bird is the *Zenaida macroura*, or mourning dove. Its name derives from its long, mournful, cooing call, which sounds something like this:

(Makes a very impressive call of the mourning dove.)

The mourning dove is a strong, fast flier that flushes up with a whirring of its wings. This first dove I bought, I named after my closest friend, Samir Saboura. We went to grade school together. While I drew birds, he made up words. He made up a word for the motion of a stone falling. *(Speaks a made-up word, with confidence)* The way a fish flicks its tail in the water. *(Another word)* The sound an apple makes when it's bit. *(Another word)* Samir Saboura. A strong fast flier that flushed up with a whirring of his wings.

My grandmother, Lak'aa Faseeh Zayer, took care of my pigeons when I was conscripted. Samir and I, we were in Saddam's army in '91, not the elite Republican Guard, but just the ordinary shock troops. What luck. What luck that we managed to stay together throughout the war. We hid in bunkers for most of those weeks. Cursing Saddam‗ when our captain was out. Cursing the Brits and the Yanks the rest of the time. And I missed my birds. But birds were prohibited in the bunkers. Prohibited. Prohibited by the laws of nations as were the fuel-air explosive bombs, the napalm—Shhhh!—the cluster and antipersonnel weapons. Prohibited, as were the BLU-82 bombs, a fifteen-thousand-pound device—Shut up!—capable of incinerating every living thing, flying or grounded, within hundreds of yards . . . And me, I missed my birds. The way they looked at me, their eyes little pieces of peace sailing my way.

After the war, I sold them one by one, all twelve of them. For food. For aspirin. I sold them. But not before I sold the watch my great-uncle gave me, the spoon my aunt gave mother, with my name inscribed the day I was born. Not before I sold my Shakespeare, in Arabic, first, then my copies in English. Because I knew. I knew. That my birds would not be shown at the next convention.

I remember. I remember. Everything we say these days begins with "I remember." Because the things we saved from the past, we sell day by day for a future in a bucket of slops and potato skins. A bunch of Dole bananas and a bag of apples from Beirut cost a teacher's salary for a month. Only the rich eat fruit. So all we can do is remember. I remember, a few months after the bombing stopped, my grandmother falling on a piece of broken pipe, her thigh cut to the bone. Little pink pills. Little pink pills of penicillin were all she needed. But these were prohibited by the blockade, prohibited for import, as are chemotherapy drugs and painkillers—not again, Ali! *(Beat)* Five thousand pigeons die a month because of this blockade. No. *(Beat)* Five thousand children die a month because of this blockade . . . I will count to five thousand and then perhaps you will see how many five thousand is. *(Slowly)* One, two, three, four, five, six, seven, eight, nine, ten, eleven, twelve, thirteen, fourteen . . . It takes a long time to count that far.

Little pink pills. That was all we needed to save Lak'aa Faseeh Zayer, my grandmother. She lay in my mother's arms, rotting from the waist down while the birds disappeared from the avenues because the trees had died. And this was the land of dates. How many dates? How many birds? The sadness of numbers is that they do not stop and there is always one more to follow. Just like birds.

(Quotes:)

> Do you ne'er think who made them, and who taught
> The dialect they speak, where melodies
> Alone are the interpreters of thought?

"The Birds of Killingworth," Henry Wadsworth Longfellow. He was one of Samir's favorites, along with al-Mutanabbi, al-Sayyab and Kanafani. And, of course, the poets of love. And what of love? What is a book on the pigeon and the dove if it does not treat the philosophies of love? I don't know *(Beat)* I don't know what love is. It goes. It comes. It goes. It comes. Samir Saboura. My friend. If love is in pieces, then he was a piece of love.

Tall, tall, he was. A handsome fellow with big dark eyes but, and I must say it, he walked like a pigeon. Now, pigeons are not really meant to walk. Their state of grace is to fly. But if they must walk, they walk like Samir walked. Like this:

(He walks like Samir, bobbing his head in and out, taking sure but awkward steps.)

It's possible his great-grandfather was a flamingo. Samir. He was intelligent and hilarious, but he had one fault: he could hardly read. He was terribly dyslexic. So we would do the reading for him. Samir was always carrying a book, and whoever he came upon, he would say, "Read to me." He'd memorize whole passages that he would recite at the most inopportune of moments. For instance, I had food poisoning when I was sixteen. All day I sat on the toilet, rocking and moaning. And, I must say it, stinking as well. But Samir would not leave my side. He would not leave me to suffer alone. Up and down the hallway outside the bathroom he strode, reciting pieces of Hart Crane. While I sputtered and farted in agony, snatches of *The Bridge* sailed in and out of my consciousness and kept me from despair:

(He quotes Samir reciting Hart Crane:)

And if they take your sleep away sometimes
They give it back again. Soft sleeves of sound
Attend the darkling harbor, the pillowed bay.

A good friend, Samir. He had a library that even his teachers envied. He couldn't read the books himself, but he slept and ate among them. Running his big hands over their spines, he would grin at us, "I cannot read them, but I can touch them." He was so intimate with his books that he could close his eyes and find a book by its smell.

(He tears a small piece of paper from a book and smells it, then eats it.)

Books can also, in extreme times, be used as sustenance. But such eating makes for a parched throat. Many mornings I wake and I am thirsty. I turn on the taps but there is no running water. A once-modern city of three million people, with no running water for years now. The toilets are dry because we have no sanitation. Sewage pools in the streets. When we wish to relieve ourselves, we squat beside the dogs. At night, we turn on the lights to read the books we have forgotten we have sold, but there is no electricity. We go to the cupboard to eat cold cans of soup but there is no food processing so the cupboards are bare. A couple of us wanted to write a few polite words of complaint to the United Nations Sanctions Committee, but it has blocked the import of pencils as it is feared they might be used for making "weapons of mass destruction." Just recently it was reported that despite the blockade, at the very tops of some of the most remote mosques, nests have been found made entirely of pencils. *(Whispers)* Stockpiling.

(He opens the book again.)

Sometimes, if the occasion is right, a book is for reading.

(He snaps the book shut. Then recites quietly:)

> Some say the world will end in fire,
> Some say ice.
> From what I've tasted of desire,
> I hold with those who favor fire.

Robert Frost. You teach that in school. 88,500 tons of bombs. Write this down without pencils: the equivalent of seven and a half atomic bombs of the size that incinerated Hiroshima. Nine hundred tons of radioactive waste spread over much of what was once the land of dates. *(He gets rid of the book)* Somewhere within this information is a lullaby.

(He sings a piece of the same Arab lullaby he learned from his grandmother. Beat.)

And this, my friends, is documented. Fact. Fact. By the European Parliament, 1991. Members of the committee recorded the testimony, drinking cups of cold coffee: the defeated troops were surrendering. We, a nation of "unpeople," were surrendering. Samir and myself, along-side seven hundred other men. We were dirty and tired and hungry, sucking orange mints because the napalm made our gums bleed. That morning, I'd relieved myself beside the others while invisible jets broke the black-glass sky across the horizon. My friend Samir did the same.

And then we walked towards the American unit to sur-render, our arms raised beside seven hundred other men.

(He raises his arms.)

Samir, he said to me—this is not documented—he said, "I want to put my hands in a bucket of cold water." Shut up, I said, keep your hands up. Samir said, "I want to smell the back of my father's neck." Shut up, I said. Shut up. We're almost home. Samir Saboura said, "I want to tell an astonishing joke until you cry for relief."

As we walked towards them—this is documented—the commander of the U.S. unit fired, at one man—an anti-

tank missile, a missile meant to pierce armor. At one man.
The rest of us, arms still raised, stopped walking. I remember. I remember.

(He slowly lowers his arms.)

I could not. I could not recognize. My friend Samir. A
piece of his spine stuck upright in the sand. His left hand
blown so high in the air it was still falling. Then they
opened fired on the rest of us.

A bullet hit me in the back as I ran. Out of hundreds,
thousands in that week, a handful of us survived. I lived.
Funny. That I am still here. The dead are dead. The living, we are the ghosts. We no longer say good-bye to one
another. With the pencils we do not have we write our
names so the future will know we were here. So that the
past will know we are coming.

(He quotes:)

> In a world that seems so very puzzling is it any
> wonder birds have such appeal? Birds are, per-
> haps, the most eloquent expression of reality.

Roger Tory Peterson, American ornithologist, born 1908.

(He quotes again:)

> War is hell.

Pete Williams, Defense Department spokesman, on con-
firming that U.S. Army earthmovers buried alive, in their

trenches, up to eight thousand Iraqi soldiers. *(Beat)* Yep. Yep. War is hell. And birds are perhaps the most eloquent expression of reality. In Arabic we say:

(In Arabic, he says the equivalent of, "Fuck that," two times.)

Which is the equivalent of, "Fuck that."

I sold my last bird a few days ago. Tomorrow I will sell the cage. The day after that I will have nothing more to sell. But I keep track of the buyers, and who the buyers sell to. I go to their homes and I ask for the bones. Usually the family is kind, or frightened of me, and they give me the bones after the meal. I boil the bones and keep them in a bucket.

(We now notice an old steel bucket elsewhere onstage. He takes the bucket.)

Listen.

(He shakes the bucket a few times. We hear the sound of bones rattling.)

It is a kind of music.

(He holds the bucket out to the audience.)

These are the bones of those who have died, from the avenue of palms, from the land of dates. I have come here to give them to you for safekeeping. *(Beat)* Catch them. If you can.

*(He throws the contents of the bucket at the audience.
Instead of bones, into the air and across the audience,
spill hundreds of white feathers.)*

THE END

One Short Sleepe

A Ten-Minute Play

PRODUCTION HISTORY

One Short Sleepe was written for The Global Play Project at The University of Iowa.

One Short Sleepe received its world premiere at the Humana Festival of New American Plays in March 2008 at the Actors Theatre of Louisville (Marc Masterson, Artistic Director; Jennifer Bielstein, Managing Director). It was directed by Marc Masterson. Ramiz Monsef played the role of Basheer.

A young Lebanese man, Basheer, early twenties, dressed casu-
ally, is digging a hole in the ground with a shovel. He digs at
different times during the scene but often breaks for periods
while speaking to us.

BASHEER: At the end of her body. Yes. At the end of her. Body.
There are six spinning fingers, called "spinnerets," which
make a spinning machine so intricate nothing can match
it. These fingers, or spinning tubes, having tiny holes at
the end of each one through which spills the thread. Spills.
I like that word. And I say "spills" as the spider's web is
actually liquid until it comes into. Contact. Into contact
with the air. On the feet are tiny claws to guide the thread,
three different kinds. And the pilots. Let me tell you about
the pilots: when they are very young they climb to the
highest points they can find and then turn to face the
wind. And there are various kinds of wind. Today, for
instance, is the kind of wind the shapes of jets leave
behind. When the jets disappear, their silver hangs in the

air, their cold fuel floats like blue threads over the city. Nothing to do with beauty, everything to do with precision. For the spider then stands on tiptoe, raises its opisthosoma, its abdomen or end, as high as it can in the air and sends out a stream of silk from its youthful spinnerets. The air takes up the thread and the spinner pays out its line until it is long enough to tug the spider, and hold its weight. Then the spider lets go—and pilots the craft through the breeze. And the spider is not at the mercy of the wind but can haul in its thread or lengthen it to rise and fall in the air.

(He lets out a celebratory call.)

This tiny, perfect aircraft may travel long distances, even out to sea, perhaps to end up on foreign soil. Or, if unlucky, to spin its thread on a wave. A wave.

That's how they came for us.

Wave after wave, the pilots, covering the ground. Covering the ground with four. Covering the ground with four million. Covering the ground with four million cluster munitions. Covering our streets, our roofs. The bomblets lay their hard fruit in the broken road. And they were made not by God, as the spiders are, but by hands: soldering, cutting, screwing, polishing, testing. And I studied. I studied. Up until the moment of spinnerets, the spiders and their wonders. Of all the studies I could have chosen at Beirut University, I chose entomology because spiders have eight eyes, arranged in two rows on the front of their heads. Eight eyes, imagine it. Eight opportunities to witness an event at a different angle.

It was summer. In the year 2006. The jets took off just outside Tel Aviv and Haifa, perhaps even Jerusalem. And my enemy, my brother the pilot, pulled the night smooth and tight across our garden while my sister Ghada examined an ant on her finger. She held the creature up to my face. "Get lost!" I said.

(He holds up the blade of the shovel and talks to it as though it were his sister:)

"Get lost, Ghada! I'm reading. I have exams tomorrow little girl! You know nothing about spiders and soon I will know everything!" We were cruel to each other, my eight-year-old sister and I, because we loved each other absolutely. I was turning the page of my book on spiders. The sirens were sounding. The leaflets were dropping. The kindness of warnings: "You are ordered to evacuate your villages immediately." We had no weapons in our home. But, ah, the wonder, the wonder of those tiny spinning tubes, of the liquid, of contact with the air.

It was the second raid. My mother couldn't get back home. She was with her mother, safe, across town. My dear father was on our roof. His legs were at the bottom of the stairs. And Ghada had an ant at the end of her body. At the end of her body, on the end of her finger. And she was singing or weeping, singing or weeping, and I told her to stop but she just kept on:

(He sings, first in Arabic, then in English:)

> Little ant, little ant,
> God lives in you.
> Take me to your home,
> The sky's no longer blue.

I said:

(He speaks to the shovel blade again:)

"Shut up. Sing about spiders, you stupid girl! Not ants. Not ants. Ants can't be pilots."
 The noise of jets is silence. Until they are done. And when they are done, grace closes its door.

(He has finished digging.)

I was going to be an expert on insects. I read all the books in English. I knew the Latin names for "silence," for "silly girls," for "the numbers that surround the number eight."
 The bomb that was falling towards our house, the bomb that was fabricated in Nevada or Wisconsin or Indiana, was dreamt into being through a good day's labor and a good day's work.
 And then we were hit.
 I wish I had been born a spider. "Chelicera." "Epigastric furrow." "Spigots." Such eloquent names for small pieces of the body. And to have eight eyes. Eight eyes to see the world from different vantage points in that half second before death, when the sky is clear as cold weather, when the sun is tiny in our throats and we kneel at our graves but cannot not warm the dirt, cannot gather our pieces again, nor explain the absence of the love of strangers whom we have never met, only what they have touched.
 My sister Ghada and I. We couldn't hold it together. No. We could not hold it together. Our bodies went in different directions. We were. Dispersed. Yes. We "kicked the bucket," we "bit the dirt," we "battened down the hatches." No. That last one is wrong. Maybe . . . "croaked"?

(He now puts down the shovel and speaks sharply to the grave he's been digging:)

Oh, it wasn't like that, was it? Hey, I've been to university, Sister. I know a thing or two. You've got no sense of humor, kid . . . Then you tell me, what were we like when we died?

(He listens to his sister's answer some moments.)

You are a brat!

(He listens again.)

All right! All right! *(Beat)* Ghada says she has eight eyes. Even though she didn't go to University. Even though she never studied spiders! And she says she saw eight things:

One: that we were, both of us, standing side by side, two clear armfuls of water.

Two: that when the bomb dropped down into us, our water leapt from its hold.

Three: that the wind caught us as our liquid made contact with the air.

Four: that we payed out our lines.

Five: we payed out our lines of gossamer thread with the time we had left to us.

Six: that there was a tug at our lines.

Seven: so we let ourselves go.

(He hesitates.)

What is the eighth thing you saw, Ghada?

(He listens.)

Huh. She says she won't tell me because I raised my voice.

(He sits on the edge of the grave and examines his work.)

I have made a good hole. Though not, perhaps, just for us. Not just for myself and Ghada.

(He listens to his sister again.)

All right. You can have one of my special ink pens if you tell me. But just one.

(He listens again.)

With the eighth eye my sister says she did not see anything. With the eighth eye in that moment she heard a song. *(To his sister)* How can you hear with an eye, silly? *(He listens)* Oh. That's how. *(To us)* Though I am forbidden to tell you. Yet. *(He winks at us)*
  But I can tell you what she says she heard.

(He listens. Then he sings:)

  Spider, spider, little boy.

(To the grave/his sister) Oh. Sorry. My ears are no longer so good from the blast.

(He speaks to us) It's not "boy." I try again:

(He sings first in English, then in Arabic:)

Spider, spider, little joy
Who lives in your eyes?

It was so long ago.
It was just yesterday.

Eight times I saw love.
Eight times love saw me.

THE END

Further Reading

Armstrong, Karen. *Islam: A Short History*. New York: Modern Library, 2002.

Chacham, Ronit. *Breaking Ranks: Refusing to Serve in the West Bank and Gaza Strip*. New York: Other Press, 2003.

Cohen, Mark R., and A. L. Udovitch, eds. *Jews Among Arabs: Contacts and Boundaries*. Princeton: Darwin Press, 1989.

Hass, Amira. *Drinking the Sea at Gaza*. London: Hamish Hamilton, 1999.

Khalidi, Rashid. *The Iron Cage: The Story of the Palestinian Struggle for Statehood*. Boston: Beacon Press, 2006.

Kushner, Tony, and Alisa Solomon, eds. *Wrestling with Zion: Progressive Jewish-American Responses to the Israeli-Palestinian Conflict*. New York: Grove Press, 2003.

Lamb, Franklin P. *The Price We Pay: A Quarter-Century of Israel's Use of American Weapons Against Civilians, 1978–2006.* Beirut: Lamont Press, 2007.

Makdisi, Saree. *Palestine Inside Out: An Everyday Occupation.* New York: W. W. Norton, 2008.

Nathan, Susan. *The Other Side of Israel: My Journey Across the Jewish-Arab Divide.* London: HarperCollins, 2005.

Pappé, Ilan. *The Ethnic Cleansing of Palestine.* Oxford: One-World Publications, 2006.

Reinhart, Tanya. *Israel/Palestine: How to End the War of 1948.* New York: Seven Stories Press, 2002.

Reuter, Christoph. *My Life Is a Weapon: A Modern History of Suicide Bombing.* Translated by Helena Ragg-Kirkby. Princeton: Princeton University Press, 2004

Rodinson, Maxime. *Israel: A Colonial-Settler State?* Translated by David Thorstad. New York: Monad Press, 1973.

Rose, Jacqueline. *The Question of Zion.* Princeton: Princeton University Press, 2005.

Rose, John. *The Myths of Zionism.* London: Pluto Press, 2004.

Roy, Sara. *Failing Peace: Gaza and the Palestinian-Israeli Conflict.* Ann Arbor: Pluto Press, 2007.

Shehadeh, Raja. *When the Bulbul Stopped Singing: A Diary of Ramallah Under Siege.* London: Profile Books, 2003.

Viswanathan, Gauri, ed. *Power, Politics, and Culture: Interviews with Edward W. Said*. New York: Pantheon Books, 2001.

Warschawski, Michel. *On the Border*. Translated by Levi Laub. Cambridge, MA: South End Press, 2005.

Weizman, Eyal. *Hollow Land: Israel's Architecture of Occupation*. London: Verso, 2007.

NAOMI WALLACE was born in Kentucky, and presently lives in North Yorkshire, England.

Wallace's major plays include *Things of Dry Hours*, *One Flea Spare*, *The Trestle at Pope Lick Creek*, *In the Heart of America*, *Slaughter City*, *The War Boys*, *The Inland Sea*, *Birdy* (an adaptation of William Wharton's novel for the stage) and *The Fever Chart: Three Visions of the Middle East*.

Wallace's work has been awarded the Susan Smith Blackburn Prize, the Fellowship of Southern Writers Drama Award, the Kesselring Prize, the Mobil Prize, an NEA grant, a Kentucky Arts Council grant, a Kentucky Foundation for Women Grant and an OBIE Award for Best Play. Wallace is also a recipient of the MacArthur Fellowship, the grant popularly known as the "genius award."

Her plays are published in Great Britain by Faber and Faber, and in the U.S. by TCG and Broadway Play Publishing. Her book of poetry *To Dance a Stony Field* is published in the U.K. by Peterloo Poets.

Her award-winning film *Lawn Dogs* was produced by Duncan Kenworthy. Her film *The War Boys* (adapted with Bruce McLeod from Wallace's play of the same name) will be released in 2010.